My
VIRGIN
DIET
RECIPES

STACY LONGORIA

LIFEVISION PUBLISHING

My
VIRGIN
DIET
RECIPES

The recipes I used to lose 17 *pounds*
In just 3 *weeks*

STACY LONGORIA

DISCLAIMER

The information provided in this book is for educational purposes only. I am not a physician and this is not to be taken as medical advice or a recommendation to stop eating other foods. The information provided in this book is based on my experiences and interpretations of the past and current research available. If you have any health issues or pre-existing conditions, please consult your doctor before implementing any of the information that is presented in this book. Cooking results may vary from individual to individual. This book is for informational purposes only and the author or publisher does not accept any responsibilities for any liabilities or damages, directly or indirectly, resulting from the use of this book.

MY NOTES

1._____

_____

2._____

_____

3._____

_____

4._____

_____

5._____

_____

6._____

_____

7._____

_____

8._____

_____

I Lost 17 Pounds in 3 Weeks!

Do you know what it's like to be loaded with belly fat and plagued with fatigue? I do! I was a serious foodie and there was absolutely no doubt about it. My love for food could easily be seen in no uncertain terms. Apart from being overweight, I had a bunch of other complaints. I had zits all over my face and back, I had severe cravings, I had inflammation problems in my body and I was literally feeling tired all day long. Clearly, I was out of line with my health and I just couldn't lose weight, so I decided to take my health seriously.

HOW IT ALL STARTED...

In what I call more than mere coincidence, I first saw JJ Virgin on an interview with *Drew Canole* of *FitLife TV*. I am now proud to declare that since then, I have fully adapted to the Virgin Diet lifestyle from January 2013. At first and quite frankly, the diet sounded really ridiculous and unworkable. For me, eliminating seven foods **(corn, gluten, peanuts, sugar, soy, dairy and eggs)** from my diet was a tough plan for a foodie like me to follow. Even though it appeared to be such a difficult concept at first, I decided to start the diet to see the results. It was challenging, but quite interesting. Three weeks later, I actually felt different—in a good way. Surprisingly, I had lost a total of 17 pounds and the zits were clearing up rather quickly. For me, this was significant progress. Excited that I had accomplished such a feat in such a short time, I started to experiment with different recipes that could fit into my newly adapted Virgin Diet lifestyle. My food enthusiasm and love for cooking propelled me even further. I started thinking about the idea of sharing my recipes with countless others around the world and the rest is history. Now, I am sharing my specially created Virgin Diet recipes with you and many others. These are some of the recipes that have helped me to shed pounds like I never did before.

In addition to losing weight, this diet has helped to heal my gut, revitalize my body with good nutrients and clear out my system. This is why I am so passionate about sharing my own Virgin Diet recipes. These are the recipes that I've used to lose weight on the Virgin Diet and the recipes are based on the diet's specific guidelines.

I have never turned back since my Virgin Diet discovery. I never will! Special thanks to JJ Virgin, she literally changed my life—for good. I am grateful that she openly shared her expertise and her research in such a profound dietary approach that will help thousands of people to lose weight, just like me.

WHAT IS THE VIRGIN DIET?
As mentioned earlier, the Virgin Diet was founded by JJVirgin. All credit is given to JJ Virgin for her hard work and brilliant expertise in regards to the Virgin Diet regime. Based on her findings, but in my own words, the Virgin Diet is basically a reactive food elimination approach to weight loss. Dieters are encouraged to avoid the high food intolerance foods. This means no corn, no gluten, no dairy, no peanuts, no harmful sugars or artificial sweeteners, no soy and no eggs. Importantly, she has structured the diet around three cycles.

Cycle 1 is the first cycle and it lasts for 21 days. During this 21 day period, the 7 highly reactive foods are eliminated from the diet.

Cycle 2 lasts for a 28 day period. Over a 4-week period dieters will customize the Virgin Diet regime by bringing back only 4 of the 7 highly reactive foods (soy, gluten, egg, and dairy) in the diet in order to see how the body reacts. This is done by reintroducing one of these 4 foods each week. By doing this, dieters will be able to determine which foods are harming them as well as which foods are contributing to their healthy lifestyle and proper weight maintenance. Note that JJ Virgin encourages dieters to avoid the other 3 highly reactive foods (harmful sugars or artificial sweeteners, peanuts, corn) altogether or only include them in the diet at a minimum. These 3 should only be included in about 5 percent of the overall diet.

Cycle 3 is the final cycle and it is about continuing on the new Virgin Diet lifestyle and staying informed about diet specific tactics that will help dieters maintain a lifetime of optimum health. For me, I just stick to the cycle 1 recipes consistently at this stage. This does not mean, however, that you have to do the same. I recommend that you stick to JJ Virgin's routine for the diet.

The bottom line is that the Virgin Diet is not just about food elimination—it's about eating healthy, wisely and getting positive health results.

WHO IS THIS DIET FOR?
Whether you are a Virgin Dieter or you basically want to eat healthier, lose weight, or overcome food intolerance, this diet should serve you well. In other words, it is created to make you win. Additionally, I believe that despite food eliminations, cooking can remain interesting and tasty. It shouldn't feel like a jail sentence. Here is where these recipes come in. Take a positive step towards your health and experience permanent weight loss and restoration with these healthy recipes. These recipes present a healthier alternative to the way people normally eat. By using these recipes week after week, soon it will be realized that it is a win-win approach. You'll find recipes for all three cycles of the Virgin Diet within the chapters, plus a helpful list of recommended food substitutes. The Cycle 1 recipes will be the most common recipes that I share, which means that all of these recipes are **Gluten-Free, Soy-Free, Egg-Free, Dairy-Free, Peanut-Free, Corn-Free and Sugar-**

Free. This is because I've come to realize that a lifestyle using the Cycle 1 recipes are the real deal breakers. By eliminating these 7 reactive foods from your daily diet, you are likely to experience optimum health.

Now, I can agree that food intolerance is one of the most significant weight gain culprits.

Cheers to your health,

CYCLE 1 BREAKFAST RECIPES

Chia Walnut Dream

If you don't want to feel like you are on a diet, this recipe is a great pick. Enjoy this walnut chia delightful dish will be prepared from overnight.

Servings: *1-2*

PREPARATION TIME: *10 minutes*

Ingredients:

- 2 tablespoons walnuts, crushed
- ½ cup pre-cooked brown rice
- 2 tablespoon chia seeds
- ½ cup organic unsweetened coconut milk
- ¼ teaspoon cinnamon powder
- ¼ teaspoon vanilla essence
- 1-2 teaspoon coconut palm sugar
- ¼ cup of your favorite berries

Directions:

1) Combine together chia seeds, cooked brown rice, unsweetened coconut milk, cinnamon powder, vanilla essence and coconut palm sugar in a bowl.
2) Place a cover on the bowl and refrigerate overnight.

3) The next morning, stir the chia mixture in the bowl and evenly distribute the ¼ cup berries and crushed walnuts on top.

4) Serve and enjoy.

Almond Thickie

This is a perfect substitute for regular oatmeal and is also virgin diet friendly.

Servings: 2

PREPARATION TIME: 10 minutes

COOKING TIME: 30 minutes

Ingredients:

- 1 cup of gluten free oatmeal
- 2 cup of organic unsweetened coconut milk
- 1 teaspoon of cinnamon
- 3 tablespoon of coconut palm sugar
- 1 teaspoon Malaysian Palm Fruit Oil
- ½ cup of almonds, chopped

Directions:

1) In a pan, heat the oil.
2) Add the oatmeal and allow to cook for about 2 minutes while stirring.
3) Pour in the coconut milk.
4) Add the spices and the almonds.
5) Frequently stir for about 25 minutes.
6) Now add the sugar and stir for another 4 minutes. Serve cold.

Coconut Breakfast Bites

Prepare these interesting breakfast bites in record time. Enjoy these almond coconut bites for a fulfilling breakfast.

Servings: *2*

PREPARATION TIME: *10 minutes*

COOKING TIME: *5-10 minutes*

Ingredients:

- ½ cup of coconut flour
- ½ cup of almond flour
- 2 tablespoon Extra-virgin Coconut Oil
- ½ cup of organic unsweetened coconut milk (add more if needed)
- 1 teaspoon of cinnamon
- 1 teaspoon of cardamom
- ½ cup of shredded coconut
- A pinch of unrefined sea salt
- 2 tablespoon of coconut palm sugar (or according to taste)

Directions:

1) In a bowl, mix all the ingredients well together.
2) Mix them with a whisk until they are smooth.
3) Now heat the oil in a pan.

4) Pour in the mixture and golden fry on both sides.

5) Optional: Sprinkle some shredded coconut on top while serving.

Morning Berry Shake

A healthy breakfast is important for boosting your health for the rest of the day. Start your day with this healthy shake and enjoy the taste while you are at it. This is an easy shake to make every as often as you wish.

Servings: *2*

PREPARATION TIME: *10 minutes*

Ingredients:

- o   1 cup of frozen strawberries
- o   ½ cup of black berries
- o   A handful of spinach
- o   ½ cup of organic unsweetened coconut milk
- o   A pinch of lime or lemon zest

Directions:

1) Pour all the ingredients into a food processor or blender.
2) Blend for about 3 minutes or until you get a wonderful smooth texture.
3) Serve fresh and enjoy.

Kale Avocado Pleasure

Kale Avocado Pleasure is perfect to have every morning due to its high nutritional benefits. It has a rich creamy texture and packed with fiber, plus healthy oils, vitamins and minerals.

Servings: 2

PREPARATION TIME: 10 *minutes*

Ingredients:

- A handful of kale
- 2 carrots, diced
- 1 teaspoon of cinnamon
- 2 tablespoon of coconut palm sugar
- 3 avocados, diced
- 2 cups of organic unsweetened coconut milk
- A pinch of unrefined sea salt

Directions:

1) In a blender, pour all the ingredients.
2) Blend for nearly about 2 minutes or until you get your desired texture.
3) Serve fresh.

Pumpkin Pudding Delight

This recipe is quite tasty and very easy to follow. Maybe this recipe will also help to add variation to your regular breakfast regime.

Servings: 2

PREPARATION TIME: *10 minutes*

COOKING TIME: *30 minutes*

Ingredients:

- o   1 cup of freshly made pumpkin puree
- o   2 cup of organic unsweetened coconut milk
- o   1 teaspoon of cinnamon
- o   1 teaspoon of cardamom
- o   1-2 tablespoons Malaysian Palm Fruit Oil
- o   3 tablespoon of coconut palm sugar

Directions:

1) In a skillet heat and add the oil.
2) Add the pumpkin puree and spices.
3) Adjust to medium to low heat and stir at intervals for 5 minutes.
4) Pour in the coconut milk and stir.
5) Cook for 15 minutes.
6) Now add the sugar and again stir for another 5 minutes.

7) Let it cool and serve cold.

Coco Berry Trail

This is a perfect breakfast recipe that is packed with healthy antioxidants. Enjoy the Coco Berry Trail.

Servings: *2*

PREPARATION TIME: *10 minutes*

Ingredients:

- o   2 apples cored, chopped
- o   ½ cup of cherries
- o   ½ cup of berries
- o   2 cup of organic unsweetened cold coconut milk
- o   4 tablespoons of chopped almonds
- o   1 teaspoon of cinnamon
- o   1 teaspoon of cardamom
- o   3 tablespoon of coconut palm sugar

Directions:

1) Heat the coconut milk for 10 minutes.
2) In a baking tray pour in the cold coconut milk, almonds, spices and sugar.
3) Add the chopped apples, and berries, cherries on top.
4) Bake for 20 minutes over 180C heat.

Mushroom Topped Spinach

Rich earthy mushrooms will bring your spinach to a gourmet level with this dish. Make this dish your mushroom breakfast special.

Servings: *2*

PREPARATION TIME: *10 minutes*

COOKING TIME: *30 minutes*

Ingredients:

- 1 Pound (453 grams) sliced baby mushrooms (portabella)
- 2 cloves of minced garlic
- ¼ cup raw coconut vinegar or other diet friendly vinegar
- 2 tablespoons purified water
- Generous pinch of dried parsley and dried thyme
- Unrefined sea salt and freshly cracked black pepper
- Extra virgin olive oil
- ½ pound (226 grams) spinach

Directions:

1) Place a thin film of oil in skillet or frying pan. On medium heat add mushrooms, unrefined sea salt and pepper. Cook about 10 minutes stirring occasionally.
2) Add garlic and continue to cook while stirring 1 – 2 minutes until garlic is fragrant.

3) Add parsley, thyme, water and vinegar or coconut aminos

4) Reduce until liquid has evaporated.

5) Place mushroom mixture in a warm bowl.

6) Re-film the pan with oil if needed. Add the spinach. Sauté until spinach about one minute, until spinach has wilted. Remove from heat.

7) Place a bed of spinach on plate then top with mushrooms.

Dates Pancake

If you love dates and want to try it in a new twist, this recipe is perfect for you.

Servings: 2

PREPARATION TIME: 10 minutes

COOKING TIME: 5 minutes

Ingredients:

- o   ½ cup of cashew nut or almond flour
- o   ½ cup of coconut flour
- o   ½ cup organic unsweetened coconut milk (add more if needed)
- o   1 tablespoon chia seeds missed with 3 tbsp water and soaked for about 15 minutes
- o   2 tablespoon of date paste (variation: use 2 tbsp coconut palm sugar)
- o   2 tablespoon Extra-virgin Coconut Oil
- o   A pinch of unrefined sea salt

Directions:

1) In a bowl, mix all the ingredients except the oil.
2) Now check whether the mixture is smooth or not.
3) When smooth, heat the oil in a pan.

4) Pour in the batter.

5) Fry golden brown on both sides.

6) Serve hot.

Zesty Red Fruit Salad

This is ready to eat after marinating for a short time, its flavors also mingle and permeate overnight to enjoy with breakfast or a side dish at lunch.

Servings: *2*

PREPARATION TIME: *10 minutes*

COOKING TIME: *10-20 minutes*

Ingredients:

- o 1 cup cherries
- o 1 cup strawberries
- o 1¼ teaspoon whole coriander seeds to taste
- o Coconut palm sugar to taste
- o Bit of lemon zest, bit of fresh lemon juice

Directions:

1) Pit all cherries cutting ¾ in half, leaving ¼ of cherries whole.
2) Trim and core strawberries, place in bowl with prepared cherries.
3) In dry skillet toast coriander seeds until fragrant. Grind in spice grinder or crush in mortar and pestle. Slowly incorporate the sugar with the coriander, sprinkle over fruit.
4) Add lemon zest toss gently. Season with a bit of lemon juice.

5) Set aside for at least 10 minutes.

6) It is ready to eat.

CHAPTER 3

CYCLE 1 LUNCH RECIPES

Rich Avocado Salsa

A very authentic and yet simple salsa recipe that is healthy and would take very little time to make.

Servings: *2*

PREPARATION TIME: *10 minutes*

COOKING TIME: *10 minutes*

Ingredients:

- 2 tomatoes, sliced into cubes
- 4 avocado, sliced into cubes
- 2 cucumber, sliced into cubes
- ½ of coconut, thinly sliced or shredded
- Fresh coriander
- 1 tablespoon of coconut palm sugar
- 1 teaspoon lime or lemon juice

Directions:

1) In a mixing bowl, throw in all of your ingredients.
2) Mix them well with a spatula.
3) Serve fresh.

Pumpkin Shrimp Picasa

This is a very simple dish with a remarkable taste!

Servings: *2*

PREPARATION TIME: *10 minutes*

COOKING TIME: *20 minutes*

Ingredients:

- o   1 Pound (453 grams) of shrimp, chopped
- o   1 pumpkin, peeled, diced
- o   4 spring onions, chopped
- o   2 red pepper, chopped
- o   Fresh coriander, chopped
- o   1 tsp of mustard seeds
- o   2 tbsp of Malaysian Palm Fruit Oil
- o   1 tsp of coconut flour
- o   6 tbsp of almond milk

Directions:

1) In a pan, add the oil.
2) Fry the onions and the shrimp.
3) Add the seeds.
4) Throw in the rest of the ingredients.

5) Stir for 5 minutes.

6) Pour in the milk and cover.

7) Cook for 15 minutes and serve with appropriate diet-friendly bread.

Mushroom Shallots

This dish has an element of surprise in it. The gentle blending of the savory and the sweet will leave you wanting more.

Servings: *2*

PREPARATION TIME: *10 minutes*

COOKING TIME: *30 minutes*

Ingredients:

- 2 tbsp coconut oil
- 1 tsp ground white pepper
- 2 tsp ground coriander
- 1 large onion, diced
- 3 shallots, diced
- 6 garlic cloves, minced
- 1 small red chili (optional)
- 3 cups mushrooms, sliced
- 2 cup organic coconut cream
- 3 cups water
- 1 cup zucchini, diced
- 1 carrot, sliced finely
- ½ tsp ground nutmeg
- 2 tsp ground turmeric

Directions:

1) Heat the coconut oil, and sauté onions until soft.
2) Mash or blend the onion, shallots, garlic and red chilli with pepper and coriander mix to a paste.
3) Cook the paste about 3 minutes until aromatic.
4) Add the mushrooms and sauté for 10 minutes.
5) Pour in the coconut cream and water, zucchini and carrot.
6) Bring to a boil, reduce heat and simmer for approximately 30 minutes, until carrots are properly cooked.
7) Season with nutmeg and turmeric
8) Serve over mashed cauliflower and garnish with fresh parsley.

Spicy Bay Shrimp

This spicy and flavorful shrimp dish will brighten your table. The spicy flavour can be tailored to your taste with an adjustment to the amount of jalapenos you add.

Servings: 2

PREPARATION TIME: *10 minutes*

COOKING TIME: *30 minutes*

Ingredients:

- o   2 teaspoons Malaysian Pam Fruit Oil
- o   1 bay leaf
- o   1 medium onion, halved and thinly sliced
- o   1 or 2 jalapeno peppers, seeded plus very thinly sliced
- o   4   cloves garlic, minced
- o   1 Pound (453 grams) of raw shrimp, completely peeled and deveined
- o   3   medium tomatoes, diced
- o   ¼ cup green olives thinly sliced
- o   1 -2 limes cut in wedges

Directions:

1) Heat oil in large skillet add bay leaf cook 1 minute.
2) Add onion, jalapenos and garlic, stir and cook for 3 minutes.

3) Add shrimp cook 3 to 4 minutes until pink.

4) Stir in tomatoes and olives, bring to a simmer cover and cook 2 to 3 minutes until tomatoes begin to break down.

5) Remove bay leaf.

6) Garnish with lime wedges. Serve hot.

Spicy Sweet Potato Mix

This recipe will have you whipping up a very simple stir fry dish in less than 25 minutes.

Servings: *2*

PREPARATION TIME: *Less than 10 minutes*

COOKING TIME: *15 minutes*

Ingredients:

- o   3 sweet potatoes, diced
- o   3 carrots, diced
- o   A handful of kale, chopped
- o   Fresh mint
- o   2 onions, diced
- o   2 tsp of unrefined sea salt
- o   2 red chilies
- o   2 tablespoon Extra-virgin Coconut Oil

Direction:

1) In a pan, heat the coconut oil.
2) Add the onions.
3) Add all the veggies.
4) Now add the chillies.
5) Stir for about 15 minutes.

6) Top it off with fresh mint.

7) Serve hot.

Avocado Shrimp Salad

Enjoy this uncommon avocado shrimp recipe with a host of benefits from the avocado which includes: anti-inflammatory, fiber and healthy fats.

Servings: *2*

PREPARATION TIME: *15 minutes*

Ingredients:

- ½ pound thawed frozen shrimp, peeled and de-veined and cooked
- 2 cups Spinach, cut into bite-size pieces and remove stems
- 3 cups Lettuce, cut into bite-sized pieces
- 1 Ripe Avocado, diced
- ½ teaspoon Ground Paprika
- ¼ teaspoon Ground Cayenne
- 2½ tablespoon Olive Oil
- 1/3 cup Lime/Lemon Juice
- 3 teaspoons Raw Coconut Vinegar
- 1 teaspoon Coconut Palm Sugar
- 1 Tomato, diced
- ½ Yellow Bell Pepper, diced

Directions:

1) <u>How to cook shrimp:</u> Season shrimp with the following: cayenne, paprika, and ¼ teaspoon olive oil in a zipper bag. Shake well in order to coat the shrimp. Let stand in the refrigerator for about 25-30 minutes.

2) Heat a non-stick skillet on medium high and add in the marinated shrimp. Cook the shrimp through, for about 4-5 minutes.

3) <u>Mix together for lime dressing:</u> lime juice, olive oil, coconut vinegar and coconut palm sugar until the sugar is melted and fluids are combined well together. Place aside.

4) In a small bowl, mix spinach and lettuce together. Garnish with yellow pepper, tomato and avocado. Arrange shrimp equally on top of the vegetables, then sprinkle the salad with lime dressing.

5) Serve and enjoy your meal.

Simple Veggie Shrimp

A wonderful dish for any night's dinner! This is also one of my favorite shrimp dish.

Servings: *2*

PREPARATION TIME: *10 minutes*

COOKING TIME: *30 minutes*

Ingredients:

- o   1 Pound (453 grams) of shrimp
- o   A handful of kale
- o   2 carrots, diced
- o   2 tomatoes, sliced
- o   2 tablespoon Malaysian Palm Fruit Oil
- o   2 tsp of unrefined sea salt

Direction:

1) In a pan, heat the oil.
2) Add the onions and stir for 1 minute.
3) Add the rest of the ingredients.
4) Stir occasionally for nearly 20 minutes.
5) Serve hot.

Sweet Chicken Delight

This is a wonderful recipe for a Sunday lunch and is suitable to serve your guests too.

Servings: *2*

PREPARATION TIME: *10 minutes*

COOKING TIME: *30 minutes*

Ingredients:

- o 2 chicken breasts cut into small pieces
- o 1 cup of organic unsweetened coconut milk
- o 6 onions, chopped
- o 2 red chilies
- o 2 tbsp of almond butter
- o 2 sweet potatoes, mashed
- o Fresh coriander
- o 1 tsp of unrefined sea salt

Direction:

1) In a pot, heat the butter.
2) Add the onions and fry for 1 minute.
3) Add the chicken and stir.
4) Add the chillies and spices.

5) Pour in the potatoes and milk.

6) Stir occasionally for about 30 minutes and serve.

Stuffed Bell Pepper Chicken

Very authentic dish and it takes less than 30 minutes to prepare.

Servings: *2*

PREPARATION TIME: *10 minutes*

COOKING TIME: *20 minutes*

Ingredients:

- o   2 chicken breast, chopped
- o   2 bell peppers (1 yellow pepper and 1 red pepper both with cut in half and seeds removed)
- o   1 tsp of black pepper
- o   1 tsp of unrefined sea salt
- o   ½ cup of green peas
- o   2 spring onions, chopped
- o   1 tbsp. of Extra-virgin Coconut Oil

Directions:

1) In a pan, fry the onions over the oil.
2) Add the chicken.
3) Throw in the peppers and peas.
4) Throw in the rest of the ingredients except the two bell peppers.
5) Now sauté for about 20 minutes.

6) Now stuff the bell pepper with the mixture and serve hot.

Creamy Spiced Shrimp

Perfect dinner recipe for your family, it will take less than 45 minutes to complete.

Servings: 2

PREPARATION TIME: 10 minutes

COOKING TIME: 25 minutes

Ingredients:

- o   1 Pound (453 grams) of shrimp
- o   1 cup of organic unsweeteed coconut milk
- o   2 tbsp of almond or cashew butter
- o   6 onions, chopped
- o   2 red chilies
- o   1 tsp of pepper
- o   1 tsp of unrefined sea salt
- o   Fresh mint

Direction:

1) In a pan, heat the butter.
2) Add the onions.
3) Add the shrimp and stir.
4) Add all of your spices and chillies.
5) Now pour in the milk.

6) Cook for nearly 25 minutes.

7) Garnish with mint and serve hot.

Spicy Lentil Soup

A very easy soup for your everyday lunch! Enjoy the bursting spicy flavor

Servings: *2*

PREPARATION TIME: *10 minutes*

COOKING TIME: *30 minutes*

Ingredients:

- o 1 Pound (453 grams) of chicken, cut into small pieces
- o 1 cup of lentil, soaked overnight
- o 2 tablespoon Extra-virgin Coconut Oil
- o 2 tsp of unrefined sea salt
- o 2 onions, diced
- o 4 red chilies,
- o 1 tsp of turmeric
- o 1 tsp of paprika
- o 1 tsp of cinnamon
- o 6 cups of water

Direction:

1) In a large pot, heat the oil.
2) Fry the onions.
3) Add the chicken.

4) Stir for about 5 minutes.

5) Throw in the lentil and stir.

6) Add all the remaining spices and the chillies.

7) Now finally add the water.

8) Cover and cook for about 30 minutes.

9) Serve as needed.

Vegetable Curry

This is a quick flavorful dish that satisfies the taste buds. The tantalizing aromas will fill your kitchen and its rich flavors plus will keep your guests glued to the kitchen.

Servings: *2*

PREPARATION TIME: *10 minutes*

COOKING TIME: *30 minutes*

Ingredients:

- o 2 tablespoon Extra-virgin Coconut Oil
- o 4 cups vegetables, fresh or frozen broccoli, carrots, snow peas, zucchini, and mushrooms
- o 1 garlic clove, minced
- o ½ teaspoon fresh ginger, grated
- o 2 tbsp curry powder
- o dash nutmeg
- o pinch of cayenne (optional for kids)
- o ½ cup organic coconut milk

Directions:

1. In a Dutch oven heat oil, add vegetables, garlic, ginger, curry powder and spices. Sauté for 5-7 minutes stirring occasionally.

2. Add coconut milk and simmer 10 minutes until vegetables are tender.

3. Serve   hot.

CYCLE 1 DINNER RECIPES

Garlicky Dill Chicken

This garlic flavored dill chicken recipe is a very healthy and mouthwatering dish. It offers essential vitamins and minerals and promotes a healthy blood sugar and blood pressure levels.

Servings: *4*

PREPARATION TIME: *15 minutes*

COOKING TIME: *30 minutes*

Ingredients:

- 1 Pound (453 grams) chicken breasts, deboned and skinless
- 2½-3 teaspoons Extra-virgin Coconut Oil
- ¼ cup green onion, chopped into fine pieces
- 3 garlic cloves, finely chopped
- 1 cup chicken broth, fat-free and reduced-sodium
- 2 teaspoons Arrowroot
- 2 tablespoons Fresh Dill, chopped and divided equally
- 1 tablespoon Lime or Lemon Juice
- Unrefined Sea Salt to taste
- Black Pepper to taste

Direction:

1) Sprinkle salt and black pepper on chicken breasts

2) In a skillet, on medium-high flame, bring about 1½ teaspoons coconut oil to heat.

3) Place the seasoned chicken breasts in the heated oil and allow to brown for about 2-3 minutes on each side. Remove browned chicken, place on a plate and set aside.

4) Lessen heat to medium and pour in the rest of the coconut oil. Add garlic and onion, and stir while it is being sautéed for a minute.

5) In a small bowl or cup, mix the following together: lime or lemon juice, arrowroot, chicken broth and ½ the amount of dill. For about 2½ -3 minutes, stir occasionally as it cooks and begins to get thicker.

6) Place the chicken that was set aside and its juices into the skillet. For another 3-4 minutes, lessen the heat to low flame and allow to boil or simmer until the chicken is properly cooked. Add more salt and black pepper to the sauce if preferred and use a spoon to pour it over the chicken.

7) Sprinkle chicken with the next ½ portion of dill and serve into equal parts. Enjoy

Rich Chia Chicken Soup

This is a unique and healthy chicken soup recipe which has a good balance of spices plus the wholesome benefits of chia seeds. Chia Seeds are rich in omega 3 and are well known for their ability to keep off hunger pangs and providing antioxidant benefits.

Servings: 4

PREPARATION TIME: 15 minutes

COOKING TIME: 35 minutes

Ingredients:

o   1 chicken breast, cut in bite sized pieces

o   1 tablespoon quinoa

o   1 tablespoon brown rice

o   3 cup low fat organic and gluten free chicken broth

o   2 tablespoon chia seeds, pre-soaked in ½ cup chicken broth for at least 20 minutes

o   1 cup fresh baby carrots, cut in bite sized pieces

o   4 stalks celery, cut in bite sized pieces

o   1 small zucchini, sliced width-wise

o   ½ cup tomatoes, diced into cubes

o   2 cups raw spinach

o   ½ teaspoon cinnamon

o   1 teaspoon cilantro

o   ½ teaspoon coriander

- o   1 teaspoon oregano
- o   1 teaspoon basil
- o   ½ teaspoon cardamom
- o   Black pepper to taste
- o   Unrefined sea salt to taste

Directions:

1) In a saucepan, on medium heat, add rice, quinoa and ½ cup chicken broth in a sauce pan and cook quinoa and rice (adding more broth if necessary) it reaches a texture that is neither firm or mushy.

2) Add pre-soaked chia seeds to the saucepan with the quinoa and rice mixture and continue to cook until crispy tender. Add more broth if necessary.

3) In a soup pot, add remaining chicken broth and bring to boiling point. Add in the following: chicken breasts, celery, baby carrots, zucchini, tomatoes and spinach. Allow to cook until tender.

4) Add the crispy tender quinoa mixture and the remaining chicken broth to the soup pot ingredients. Continue cooking and you may add more water to get the consistency that you prefer.

5) Add in the remaining seasonings/spices and you may make adjustments to suit your taste.

6) Serve equally in soup bowls. Enjoy.

Salmon with Spinach and Brown Rice

This very interesting and flavorful salmon recipe is very nutritious. Coupled with the rich omega fatty acids in the salmon, you'll also get Vitamin A, Vitamin C, fiber, potassium and beta carotene nutrients from this meal. If you can't get nectarine, you may substitute it for peaches.

Servings: 2

PREPARATION TIME: 15 minutes

COOKING TIME: Under 30 minutes

Ingredients:

- 10 ounces (2 pieces or 283 grams) salmon fillet, skinless
- ½ cup brown rice
- ¾ teaspoon Extra-virgin olive oil
- 1 whole lime, peel grated
- 1 Lime, cut into wedges for garnishing
- 1 tablespoon lime/lemon juice
- 1½ small yellow pepper, sliced thinly
- ½ medium white onion, finely chopped
- ½ cup fresh basil leaves
- 3 ounces baby spinach
- 3 tablespoons water
- Unrefined sea salt to taste
- Black pepper to taste

Directions:

1) Cook brown rice according to package instructions.

2) Season salmon with about ¼ teaspoon salt and about 1/8 teaspoon black pepper. Place aside.

3) On medium heat, for about a minute, heat ¼ teaspoon olive oil in a nonstick skillet. Add seasoned salmon to skillet and cook for about 5 minutes on each side or until cooked. Remove cooked salmon and place onto a serving platter. Sprinkle grated lime peel over salmon.

4) Drain any remaining oil from skillet. On medium heat, bring ½ teaspoon olive oil to heat ½ for about a minute. Add the following ingredients: white onion, yellow pepper, water, and about 1/8 teaspoon salt. Cook covered for 4-5 minutes, then remove cover and allow to cook for another 4 minutes while stirring intermittently. Mix in basil leaves and cook until they appear wilted. Add lime/lemon juice into the mixture.

5) In another skillet or saucepan, on medium heat add about 1 teaspoon olive oil, spinach and a pinch salt. Place lid on saucepan or skillet and allow to cook for about 8 minutes while stirring occasionally or until cooked. Evenly serve the cooked spinach next to salmon, along with rice and pepper mixture. Garnish with lime wedges.

Crunchy Curried Chicken with Rice

Almonds are the hearts friend and are also full of fiber, potassium, magnesium and vitamin E. With this crunchy chicken recipe, you'll be giving your heart what it really deserves and adding well needed fibre to your diet.

Servings: 4

PREPARATION TIME: *15 minutes*

COOKING TIME: *15-20 minutes*

Ingredients:

- ½ cup raw almonds, chopped
- 1 pound (453 grams) chicken breasts, deboned, skinless and cut into 1-inch cubes
- 1-1½ cups chicken broth, fat-free and reduced-sodium
- 2 tablespoon arrowroot
- 1 tablespoon curry powder
- 1 large carrot, washed, peeled and thinly cut into slices
- 1 small red bell pepper, seed removed and thinly sliced
- 3 green onions, cut into 1-inch pieces
- Unrefined sea salt, to taste
- 2 cups brown rice, cooked and steamy
- Vital Choice Macadamia Nut Oil

Direction:

1) Prepare a non-stick skillet with Vital Choice macadamia nut oil.

2) Toast almonds: Place almonds in a medium skillet over medium-high heat for about 2 minutes and place aside.

3) In a medium bowl whisk together broth, curry powder and arrowroot and place aside.

4) Place prepared skillet over medium-high heat. Allow to warm (not steamy hot), then add chicken. For about 4-5 minutes, stir the chicken at intervals until it becomes perfectly browned (should have a golden color).

5) Add in the bell peppers, green onions and carrot while stirring to combine well. Continue to stir at intervals for another 2-2½ minutes.

6) Add in the curry mixture to the pot ingredients and allow it to reach boiling point. Lessen the heat to medium or medium-low, then place a lid on the pot and stir at intervals until sauce gets thicker and the chicken and vegetables is crunchy-cooked for another 4-5 minutes.

7) Add salt to adjust taste.

8) Evenly divide and serve cooked brown rice and curried chicken into plate. Enjoy.

Creamy Spinach Mushroom Soup

Try this powerfully healthy soup today! It's not only creamy but also delicious.

Servings: *2*

PREPARATION TIME: *10 minutes*

COOKING TIME: *30 minutes*

Ingredients:

- 2 cup of organic unsweetened coconut milk
- 4 tbsp of almond butter
- 1 cup of white mushroom, chopped
- A handful of spinach
- 1 tsp of white pepper
- 1 tsp of allspice
- 1 tsp of Malaysian Palm Fruit Oil
- 1 tsp of Monkfruit Sugar or Coconut Palm Sugar

Directions:

1) In a large pan, pour in the oil.
2) Fry the mushrooms for 2 minutes.
3) Fry the spinach for 1 minute.
4) Add the rest of the ingredients one by one.
5) Cover and cook for 25 minutes.

6) Before taking off the heat pour the sugar.

7) Serve hot.

Cinnamon Roasted Chicken

This very different chicken recipe is one of the best meals for helping to balance blood sugar levels. Cooking it in the oven is a very healthy option which contributes to the rich succulent taste.

Servings: *4*

PREPARATION TIME: *15 minutes*

COOKING TIME: *45 minutes*

Ingredients:

- o   5 small chicken thighs
- o   ¼ teaspoon cinnamon
- o   1 teaspoon paprika powder
- o   1 teaspoon black pepper
- o   3 tablespoons basil leaves
- o   1 teaspoon unrefined sea salt (or to taste)
- o   1 tablespoon Extra-virgin olive oil

Directions:

1) Preheat your oven to 375 degrees Fahrenheit. Prepare a roasting pan that is large enough to fit the chicken.

2) Combine the following in a medium-large bowl: chicken thighs, salt, olive oil, cinnamon, basil leaves, paprika powder and black pepper.

3) Put the seasoned chicken thighs in the prepared roasting pan with the skin side down. Allow to roast about 22 minutes, then turn the skin side up and continue to roast for another 20-24 minutes.

4) Serve equally and enjoy. Note: do not leave the chicken in the oven unless the oven is completely cool.

Spicy Green Peas Chicken Breasts

Treat yourself with a very fancy chicken dish today. This will serve as a delicious meal.

Servings: 2

PREPARATION TIME: 20 minutes

COOKING TIME: 20 minutes

Ingredients:

- 1 cup of organic unsweetened coconut milk
- 2 tbsp of cashew butter
- 2 chicken breasts
- 1 cup of green beans, chopped
- 4 spring onions, chopped
- ½ cup of asparagus, chopped
- ½ cup of shredded coconut
- 2 tbsp of extra virgin olive oil
- 2 chilies, chopped
- 2 tbsp of garlic paste
- 1 clove
- 1 bay leaf
- Unrefined sea salt to taste

Directions:

1) In a pan, heat the oil and fry the beans.

2) Add the chillies and asparagus.

3) Throw in the shredded coconut and stir for 5 minutes.

4) Now split the chicken breast and pour in the beans mixture onto it.

5) Seal the edges carefully by pressing it tight.

6) In another pan, heat the butter.

7) Fry the onions and add the bay leaf, the clove and all the spices.

8) Now pour in the coconut milk and add the chicken.

9) Cook for 20 minutes and serve hot.

Chicken Frita

A complete moist flavorful chicken meal with little preparation time. An easy cleanup is also an added bonus.

Servings: *2*

PREPARATION TIME: *10 minutes*

COOKING TIME: *30 minutes*

Ingredients:

- 2 chicken breasts, boneless, skinless
- 2 teaspoons extra virgin olive oil
- 6 cloves garlic, peeled
- ½ onion, sliced thin
- 1½ medium thinly sliced carrots (or 1 large),
- 1 medium sweet potato, peeled and sliced thin
- 1 sliced tomato
- 1 teaspoon dried herb of your choice
- 2 tablespoons gluten free Chicken Stock or Broth
- Unrefined sea salt and black pepper, to taste

Directions

1) Preheat oven to 350°Fahrenheit.
2) In a 9"x13" baking pan place a 2 1/2 foot long piece of foil.
3) Lightly brush top of foil with oil.

4) Add salt and pepper to chicken breast and place salted and peppered chicken breast in center of foil side by side.

5) Dip garlic cloves in oil and place 3 cloves on each breast.

6) Cover garlic topped chicken breasts with onion, carrots and potato (in that order).

7) Top with tomato slices.

8) Sprinkle top with dried herbs.

9) Drizzle oil and wine over the top.

10) Tightly wrap foil over chicken and vegetable mixture seal up well. Bake for 1 hour. Cut into center of chicken to make sure chicken is cooked throughout. Serve hot with some of the cooking juices drizzled over the top.

Virgin Shrimp Almond

Take your simple shrimp and fry it to a whole new level by adding almonds to it.

Servings: *2*

PREPARATION TIME: *10 minutes*

COOKING TIME: *30 minutes*

Ingredients:

- 1 Pound (453 grams) shrimp
- 1 cup of almonds
- 4 onions, diced
- 4 red chilies
- 1 tsp of cinnamon
- 1 tsp of cumin
- 1 tsp of paprika
- 1 tbsp of coconut palm sugar
- 2 tablespoon Extra-virgin Coconut Oil
- 1 tsp of unrefined sea salt
- Fresh mint

Direction:

1) In a pan, heat the nut oil.
2) Add the onions, almonds and stir.

3) Add the chillies and the spices.

4) Throw in the shrimp.

5) Stir for 10 minutes.

6) Add the sugar and stir for another 2 minutes.

7) Serve with fresh mint on top.

Olive Brussels

With a few ingredients and very little preparation time this dish will round out any balanced meal. It compliments lamb, chicken or fish main courses.

Servings: *2*

PREPARATION TIME: *10 minutes*

COOKING TIME: *30 minutes*

Ingredients:

- o   1 Pound (453 grams) Brussels sprouts
- o   3 tablespoons Extra-virgin olive oil
- o   1 tsp. unrefined sea salt
- o   ½ tsp. freshly ground black pepper

Directions:

1) Preheat oven 400 degrees F (205 degrees C).

2) Wash brussels sprout in cold running water.

3) Trim ends and yellow leaves.

4) Place the ingredients in a resealable Ziploc plastic bag, seal and shake to coat.

5) Pour unto baking sheet, place in preheated oven for 30-45 minutes.

6) Shake baking sheet every 5- 7 minutes for even browning.

7) Brussels sprouts should be dark brown.

8) Serve immediately.

Lamb Bells

Take your favorite ingredient lamb and give it a new spin with this recipe.

Servings: *2*

PREPARATION TIME: *10 minutes*

COOKING TIME: *20 minutes*

Ingredients:

- 1 Pound (453 grams) of lamb, cut into little slices
- 8 onions, diced
- 4 bell peppers, diced
- 1 cinnamon stick
- 1 bay leaf
- 2 tsp of unrefined sea salt
- 1 tsp of cumin
- 2 tbsp of garlic ginger paste or 1 tsp garlic and 1 tsp onion, minced
- 2 tablespoon Extra-virgin Coconut Oil
- 2 tbsp of lime or lemon juice
- Fresh coriander, chopped
- Spring onions, chopped

Direction:

1) In a pan, heat the oil.

2) Add the bay leaf and cinnamon stick.

3) Add the onions.

4) Add all the spices.

5) Throw in the lamb.

6) Now keep stirring occasionally for 20 minutes and serve hot

Spaghetti Squash Chicken Toss

Spaghetti squash is a versatile vegetable that can be used in most pasta dishes. Its mild flavor blends well with an array of sauces. This recipe is one of my favorites as well. Served with a mixed green salad it becomes a complete meal.

Servings: 2

PREPARATION TIME: *10 minutes*

COOKING TIME: *30 minutes*

Ingredients:

- o 1 large spaghetti squash
- o 1 Pound (453 grams) cherry tomatoes, each cut into quarter pieces
- o ½ cup loosely packed fresh basil leaves and thinly sliced
- o 1 cup chopped cooked chicken
- o 1 tablespoon drained capers, coarsely chopped
- o 1 tablespoon extra virgin olive oil
- o ½ teaspoon unrefined sea salt
- o ¼ teaspoon ground black pepper
- o Basil leaves for garnishing, optional

Directions

1) Cut the spaghetti squash in half from top to bottom. Remove and discard all the seeds from the inside. Rub oil on the inside and rim of the spaghetti squash. Place face down on baking sheet. Bake at 350 degrees for approximately 45 - 50 minutes.

2) While squash is baking mix remaining ingredients in a bowl.

3) Remove squash from oven allow to cool until it can be easily handled. Use a fork to scrape into spaghetti-like strands. Place squash strands into large bowl pour oil and vegetable mixture on top of squash and lightly toss until coated.

Zesty Salmon Bites

Simple and quick salmon with the amazing lime flavor.

Servings: 2

PREPARATION TIME: 10 minutes

COOKING TIME: 10 minutes

Ingredients:

- o 2 salmon pieces, deboned
- o 2 tbsp of lime juice
- o 1 tsp of cinnamon
- o 1 tsp of cumin
- o 1 tsp of paprika
- o 1 tbsp of coconut palm sugar
- o 2 tablespoon Extra-virgin Coconut Oil
- o 1 tsp of unrefined sea salt
- o Fresh Parsley

Direction:

1) Marinate the salmon with lime juice, spices, sugar and salt.
2) Heat the oil.
3) Now golden fry the salmon from both sides.
4) Serve with fresh parsley on top.

Parsley Lemon Shrimp

Try this absolutely mouthwatering shrimp recipe for a bursting spicy flavor. This is good enough to keep you making it over and over again and promotes a healthy blood pressure level.

Servings: *4*

PREPARATION TIME: *15 minutes*

COOKING TIME: *10 minutes*

Ingredients:

1 pound (453 grams) large shrimp, deveined and shells removed

1 tablespoon Malaysian Palm Fruit Oil

5 garlic cloves, minced

1 dried red chili

1 teaspoon lemon juice

1 tablespoon fresh parsley, chopped

Unrefined sea salt to taste

Directions:

1) In a saucepan, heat the palm oil over medium-high heat and cook garlic for approximately 2 minutes.

2) Add in the shrimp and chili and allow to cook through for about 4-5 minutes. Pour in lemon juice and continue to cook for another minute.

3) Turn off heat and add salt to taste and the parsley. Serve equally (about 5 shrimps each) and enjoy.

Rice 'n' Lentil Chicken

This dish brings out so many flavors all at once. Enjoy the taste while you also get good nutrition from this dish.

Servings: 2

PREPARATION TIME: 10 minutes

COOKING TIME: 30 minutes

Ingredients:

- o 2 chicken breasts cut into small pieces
- o 1 cup of brown rice, soaked
- o 1 cup of lentil, soaked
- o 4 onions, diced
- o 1 tsp of unrefined sea salt
- o 4 red chilies
- o 1 tsp of cinnamon
- o 1 tsp of cumin
- o 1 tsp of paprika
- o 2 tablespoon Extra-virgin Coconut Oil

Direction:

1) In a pressure cooker add all of your ingredients.
2) Give them a good stir.
3) Cover the lead and cook on low heat for 30 minutes.

4) Release the pressure and serve hot.

Tomato Eggplant Stew

Served on a bed of brown rice, this dish satisfies the deepest hunger pang. He will be satisfied and you will be happy knowing you cooked a healthy meal.

Servings: 2

PREPARATION TIME: 10 minutes

COOKING TIME: 30 minutes

Ingredients:

- o   2 small eggplants
- o   2 tbsp extra virgin olive oil
- o   1 chopped onion
- o   1½ cups tomato paste puree
- o   ½ cup of chickpeas, soaked over night
- o   ½ cup water

Directions

1) Dice peeled eggplant (1/2 inch cubes). Toss with 1 tsp salt. Place in colander, allow it to sweat for 20 minutes, and then pat dry.

2) In a Dutch oven, heat oil, add onions and eggplant stir and cook for 8 minutes until soft.

3) Stir in tomato sauce, chickpeas and ½ cup water. Simmer for 12 minutes until eggplant is tender. Season with black pepper. Serve over brown rice (recipe follows).

Brown Rice

In small saucepan bring 1½ cups brown rice and 1½ cups of slightly salted water to boil. Reduce heat and cover for 25 minutes until water is absorbed. Let it stand for 10 minutes. Fluff with fork before serving.

Go Easy Slow Cooker Chicken

Put your slow cooker to work while you are at work. Free your time to do all the other things on your to-do list and still have time for a delicious hot meal.

Servings: *2*

PREPARATION TIME: *10 minutes*

COOKING TIME: *30 minutes*

Ingredients:

- o   1 Pound (453 grams) whole chicken
- o   Natural poultry seasoning to taste
- o   Unrefined sea salt and pepper to taste
- o   1 teaspoon paprika

Directions

1) If your slow cooker does not have an insertive rack, place threes balls of aluminium foil (3-4 inches diameter) on the bottom of your slow cooker to allow chicken to drain as it cooks.

2) Rinse chicken inside and out under cool tap water. Pat to dry well.

3) Season chicken with salt, pepper and paprika.

4) Place in slow cooker on high for 1 hour.

5) Reduce heat setting to low for 8 hours or until chicken is no longer pink and juices run clear.

6) Carefully remove chicken from cooker, place on platter and serve with your favourite side dishes.

Coconut Tomato Soup

Bring back childhood memories with a bowl of homemade tomato soup. This soup is versatile enough that you can personalize it with your favorite toppings.

Servings: 2

PREPARATION TIME: 10 minutes

COOKING TIME: 30 minutes

Ingredients:

- o   4 tablespoons extra virgin olive oil
- o   2 medium onions, thinly sliced
- o   1 teaspoon unrefined sea salt, to taste
- o   3 teaspoons curry powder
- o   1 teaspoon ground coriander
- o   1 teaspoon ground cumin
- o   ½ teaspoon red pepper flakes
- o   2 cup tomato puree
- o   1 cup organic unsweetened coconut milk
- o   6 cups water

Directions:

1) Heat oil in a large pot. Add the onions and salt, and cook, stirring occasionally about 10 minutes just so they are tender but not brown.

2) Add curry powder, coriander, cumin, and red pepper flakes, stirring constantly for just 30 seconds or so. Add the tomato puree and 6 cups of water. Cook for approximately 12-15 minutes.

3) Using a hand blender puree until smooth. To reach the consistency you like add coconut milk or water slowly while mixing until the thickness and creaminess is to your preference. Add unrefined sea salt and pepper according to your taste.

Lemon Herbed Roasted Chicken

This is naturally delicious. Any leftovers can be used in salads or soups the next day. It's lightly seasoned flavor will enhance any dish you add it to.

Servings: 2

PREPARATION TIME: 10 minutes

COOKING TIME: 30 minutes

Ingredients:

- o   2 teaspoons Italian seasoning
- o   ½ teaspoon unrefined sea salt
- o   ½ teaspoon mustard powder
- o   4 cloves of minced garlic
- o   ½ teaspoon ground black pepper
- o   1 Pound (453 grams) whole chicken
- o   2 lemons
- o   1 tablespoons Malaysian Palm Fruit Oil

Directions

1) Preheat oven to 350 degrees F (175 degrees C).

2) Mix the seasoning salt, Italian seasoning, garlic, mustard powder, and black pepper; set aside.

3) Rub chicken with mixture both inside and out in a 9x13 inch baking dish.

4) Whisk lemon juice from 2 lemons with oil and drizzle over seasoned chicken.

5) Bake for 1½ hours, or until juices run clear, basting every 15 – 20 minutes.

6) Remove from oven let rest 10 –15 minutes before carving.

Rosemary Lamb Chops

Raise the bar at your dinner table with these aromatic lamb chops. Served with your healthy side dishes these lamb chops will give you a well-rounded dinner.

Servings: *2*

PREPARATION TIME: *10 minutes*

COOKING TIME: *30 minutes*

Ingredients:

- o   2 lamb chops (about 4 oz each)
- o   3 cloves garlic, minced
- o   2 tsp. rosemary, minced
- o   1-2 tablespoons of extra virgin olive oil
- o   Unrefined sea salt and pepper to taste

Directions

1) Preheat oven to bake at 375.
2) Pulse the rosemary and garlic until finely minced in a food processer
3) Rinse lamb under cool water and pat dry.
4) Sprinkle both sides of the chops with salt and pepper.
5) Press garlic/rosemary mixture onto both sides of lamb chops to evenly coat.

6) Bake 10 minutes on each side flipping only once.

Roasted Red Pepper Hummus

Why buy store bought hummus when it is easy to make at home with your food processor and a few ingredients. If you have five minutes you can have homemade hummus.

Servings: *2*

PREPARATION TIME: *10 minutes*

COOKING TIME: *30 minutes*

Ingredients:

- o   1 16-oz. garbanzo beans, drained
- o   Juice of one lemon
- o   2 tbsp. nut butter
- o   4 cloves garlic
- o   1/3 cup roasted red peppers
- o   3 tablespoons extra virgin olive oil
- o   2 tablespoons basil or parsley or basil chopped
- o   Unrefined Sea salt, to taste

Directions:

1) Place all ingredients in a food processer until smooth and creamy. Chill covered until ready to use.

2) Tip: Hummus is a great dip for fresh vegetables.

Grilled Shrimp

Backyard barbeques are not limited to burgers and hotdogs. Impress your family and friends with these mouthwatering shrimps.

Servings: 2

PREPARATION TIME: 10 minutes

COOKING TIME: 30 minutes

Ingredients:

- o ¼ cup extra-virgin coconut oil
- o ¼ cup lemon juice
- o 3 tablespoons chopped fresh parsley
- o 1 tablespoon minced garlic
- o Ground black pepper to taste
- o Crushed red pepper flakes to taste (optional)
- o 1 Pound (453 grams) medium shrimp, peeled and deveined
- o Unrefined sea salt to taste

Directions

1) Whisk together the extra virgin olive oil, lemon juice, parsley, garlic, crushed red pepper flakes, sea salt to taste and black pepper. Add shrimp, and mix to coat. Place in the refrigerator for 30 minutes.

2) Heat grill to high. Slide shrimp onto skewers, pierce near the tail and the head.

3) Remaining marinade should be discarded.

4) Lightly brush grill with oil.

5) Grill for 2 to 3 minutes on each side until opaque.

Italian Style Fish fillets

There is more to Italian food than pasta. These tender fish fillets will satisfy anyone.

Servings: 2

PREPARATION TIME: 10 minutes

COOKING TIME: 30 minutes

Ingredients:

- o   2 tablespoons Extra-virgin Coconut Oil
- o   1 onion, thinly sliced
- o   2 cloves garlic, minced
- o   1½ cup diced tomatoes
- o   ½ cup black olives, pitted and sliced
- o   1 tablespoon chopped fresh parsley
- o   ½ cup vegetable broth
- o   1 Pound (453 grams) cod fillets

Directions

1) In a large skillet heat oil on medium heat. Cook sliced onions and minced garlic in oil until tender.
2) Add tomatoes, olives, parsley, and wine. Cook over low heat for 5 minutes.

3) Add fillets in skillet. Simmer an additional 5 minutes, or until fish turns white.

4) Remove fish with slotted spatula place on serving dish topped with cooking sauce.

Apple Pork Chops

Savory and sweet, these pork chops will melt in your mouth. Even your children will want seconds.

Servings: 2

PREPARATION TIME: 10 minutes

COOKING TIME: 30 minutes

Ingredients:

- 4 (3/4 inch) thick pork chops
- 1 teaspoon Extra-virgin Coconut Oil
- 2 tablespoons coconut palm sugar
- Unrefined sea salt and pepper to taste
- 1/8 teaspoon ground cinnamon
- 1/8 teaspoon ground nutmeg
- 2 tablespoons extra virgin coconut Oil
- 2 tart apples - peeled, cored and sliced
- 3 tablespoons pecans (optional)

Directions:

1) Place oven proof dish in a preheated warm oven 175 degrees Fahrenheit.
2) Lightly brush chops with oil and place in a hot skillet over medium-high heat. Cook 5 to 6 minutes on each side turning

occasionally until done. Keep chops warm on the dish in the preheated oven.

3) In a small bowl, combine coconut palm sugar, salt and pepper, cinnamon and nutmeg. In the same skillet add coconut Oil, and stir in seasoned sugar mixture and apples. Cook covered until apples are almost tender. Remove apples with a slotted spoon and place on top of chops in the warm preheated oven.

4) Cook remaining sauce in skillet uncovered to thicken slightly. Drizzle sauce on apples and pork chops. Garnish with pecans.

5) Serve immediately.

Easy Garlic & Thyme Roasted Chicken

There's nothing like the bursting flavor that thyme gives to meat, especially chicken. Thyme is even one of those simple herbs that have a combination of anti-parasitic, antioxidant, anti-septic, anti-viral, anti-fungal and anti-rheumatic properties, which make this chicken recipe a sure winner. The garlic in this recipe is known to have strong antibiotic properties while supporting a healthy heart and immune system.

Servings: 4

PREPARATION TIME: 15 minutes

COOKING TIME: 1¼ hour

Ingredients:

o   1 (about 4 pounds or 1.8 kg) roasting chicken, rinsed thoroughly and patted dry
o   1 tablespoon dried thyme leaves
o   7 garlic cloves, peeled and cut in halves
o   ½ teaspoon unrefined sea salt (or to taste)
o   ½ teaspoon black pepper

Direction:

1) Preheat your oven to 375 degrees Fahrenheit. Prepare your favorite roasting pan.

2) Pierce the chicken with small piercings all over and stuff the piercings with 2-3 garlic halves and about ½ tablespoon of thyme leaves.

3) Combine the remaining ingredients in a small bowl and rub the mixture in the chicken cavity and on the skin.

4) Place the seasoned chicken in the roasting pan with a wire rack in the oven. Allow to roast for about 1¼ hours, or until the chicken is cooked. Remove the skin from the chicken, serve equally and enjoy.

Lemony Zucchini Chicken

This sautéed chicken recipe is made with vegetables that are especially antioxidant-rich and full of Vitamin C. Additionally, this ideal low-fat recipe doesn't only taste good, but it also delivers great health benefits to the heart, cells, prostate, eyes, colon and bones.

Servings: *2*

PREPARATION TIME: *15 minutes*

COOKING TIME: *30 minutes*

Ingredients:

- 2 chicken breast halves, skinless and deboned
- 2 large zucchinis cut into pieces of ¼ -inch thickness and 2-inch lengths
- 1 yellow squash, cut into pieces of ¼ -inch thickness and 2-inch lengths
- 2½ tablespoons Extra-virgin Coconut Oil
- 2 teaspoons of poultry seasoning (gluten-free)
- 1½ teaspoon garlic cloves, finely minced
- ¼ cup cilantro leaves, finely minced
- ½ cup fresh parsley leaves, finely minced
- ½ cup scallion, finely minced
- 2½ fresh ripe tomatoes, diced into ¼ -inch cubes
- 1 fluid ounce purified water
- ¼ cup lemon juice (lime juice can also be used)

- o 1 tablespoon paprika powder
- o ½ teaspoon black pepper
- o 1 Pinch unrefined sea salt

Direction:

1) In a bowl, mix together the following: scallion, salt, black pepper, tomatoes and cilantro. Set aside this tomato mix.

2) Mix the poultry seasoning, parley and paprika together and use to season the chicken breast halves.

3) In a saucepan or skillet, sauté the olive and garlic until the aroma of the garlic becomes stronger. Do not allow the garlic to burn.

4) Add the seasoned chicken breast halves to the garlic and olive oil mixture, combine well, then add purified water or grape juice.

5) Allow the chicken to cook until almost done or about 75 percent cooked through (about 3 minutes on each side). Next, add yellow squash, zucchini, and lemon juice. Cover with a lid and allow to cook until vegetables reach preferred doneness.

6) After the chicken breast halves start to reach a light brown-caramel appearance, remove along with vegetables from the pan.

7) Serve evenly, the chicken breast and vegetables in your favorite plate and top with preferred amount of tomato mix. Happy eating!

Hearty Bean and Carrot Chicken

Enjoy this fiber-rich and Vitamin A Chicken dish which is also a great low-calorie value. This is a great treat for the heart and also a quick and easy meal to make.

Servings: 4

PREPARATION TIME: 15 minutes

COOKING TIME: 30 minutes

Ingredients:

- 1 cup fresh green beans, washed and ends trimmed
- 1 pound (16 ounces or 453 grams) chicken breast halves, deboned and skinless
- ¼ teaspoon pepper
- 1 tablespoon rosemary leaves
- 1 tablespoon Extra-virgin Coconut Oil
- ¼ cup lime juice
- ½ pounds (8 ounces) baby carrots
- 6 cups water

Direction:

1) In a pot, bring 6 cups of water to a vigorous boil. Add the green beans and carrots and allow to cook for 4-5 minutes, then drain off excess water and place separately aside.

2) In a sauce pan or skillet, heat coconut oil over medium flame. Add chicken breasts and cook on each side for about 5-6 minutes.

3) Add in the green beans, carrots and the left over ingredients EXCEPT the lime juice into the sauce pan.

4) Reduce the heat to low flame and allow to cook for another 5 minutes. Add lime juice and serve equally and enjoy.

Asparagus Chicken in Coconut Sauce

This is a perfect dish for a quick, tasty and nutritious meal. Apart from the rich flavor and fiber content, this recipe also has great cancer-fighting plus anti-aging benefits.

Servings: *4*

PREPARATION TIME: *15 minutes*

COOKING TIME: *40 minutes*

Ingredients:

- o 1 pound (16 ounces or 453 grams) chicken tenderloin (Tenders), cut into bite sizes
- o 2 tablespoons Extra-virgin Coconut Oil, divided into 2 parts
- o 1 medium green onion, finely chopped
- o 3 garlic cloves, finely chopped
- o 1½ teaspoons ground cumin, divided into 2 parts
- o 1½ teaspoons ground fennel , divided into 2 parts
- o 1 small fresh chilli, seeds removed and finely chopped
- o 1 tablespoon fresh ginger, grated or finely chopped
- o 1½ pounds asparagus, cut into 1-inch pieces with woody ends trimmed
- o ½ cup of organic unsweetened coconut milk
- o ½ cup fresh cilantro, finely chopped
- o ¾ teaspoon unrefined sea salt, divided into 2 parts

Direction:

1) In a bowl, season chicken with ¼ teaspoon salt, ¾ teaspoon fennel and ¾ teaspoon cumin.

2) In a non-stick skillet or sauce pan, heat 1 tablespoon coconut oil over medium-high heat. When heated add the seasoned chicken and allow to cook until browned while stirring occasionally for 3½ minutes. Transfer the partly cooked chicken to a plate and set aside.

3) Lessen the heat to medium and pour in the following: the remaining coconut oil, chilli, garlic, ginger and onion. Allow to cool for about 3 minutes while stirring occasionally.

4) Add trimmed asparagus, sprinkle with the remaining fennel and cumin and cook for another 2 minutes while stirring occasionally.

5) Add in the remaining salt and the coconut milk and allow to simmer for another 2 minutes. Return the chicken that was set aside and any of its juices to the skillet and cook for a final 2 minutes until the chicken is properly cooked and the asparagus is crunchy and soft. Garnish with cilantro and serve equally.

Cranapple Chicken Thighs

Cranberry and apples are the highlights of this dish, which adds a naturally sweet and spicy flavor to the chicken. Enjoy the Vitamin C and antioxidant benefits of this well balanced meal. Also, enjoy the flavonoids, anti-bacterial and urinary tract benefits that come from the cranberries.

Servings: *4*

PREPARATION TIME: *15 minutes*

COOKING TIME: *20 minutes*

Ingredients:

- 1 pound (453 grams) chicken thighs, washed and nicely trimmed
- 2 fresh red apples, thinly sliced
- 1 large red onion, quartered and thinly sliced
- 1 teaspoon lemon juice
- ¾ cup gluten free chicken stock or broth, separated
- 1 cup fresh cranberries
- ¾ teaspoon dried thyme leaves, divided into 2 parts (1/4 and ½ teaspoons)
- ¾ teaspoon unrefined sea salt, divided into 2 parts
- ¼ teaspoon freshly ground pepper
- 2 tablespoons Extra-virgin Coconut Oil, divided into 2 parts
- 1 tablespoon arrowroot

Direction:

1) Season both sides of chicken thighs with salt, ground pepper and ¼ teaspoon thyme.

2) In a large skillet or saucepan, heat 1 tablespoon coconut oil on medium-high flame. Lessen heat to medium and add in the seasoned chicken. Allow the chicken to cook for about 4 minutes until browned on all sides while stirring occasionally. Remove partly chicken and place on a plate.

3) To the skillet, add the remaining 1 tablespoon olive oil, 2 chicken stock or broth, salt, onion, remaining thyme and apples. Mix together. Allow to cook for about 4 minutes while stirring regularly until the apples and onion are succulent.

4) Add in the fresh cranberries and sprinkle the pot contents with arrowroot. Continue to cook for another minute while stirring occasionally.

5) Bring back the partly cooked chicken to the skillet and add in the lemon juice and remaining chicken stock or broth. For a final 3 minutes, cover with a lid and cook while stirring every 1 minute until the sauce becomes thicker and the chicken is properly cooked.

6) Serve in equal portions and enjoy.

Spinach Greens with Oregano Grilled Chicken

This meal perfectly balances protein with iron, antioxidants, Vitamin C, Vitamin A and more. Try this quick and healthy meal that contains Spinach which is a friend to the eyes, the heart and the brain.

Servings: *4*

PREPARATION TIME: *15 minutes*

COOKING TIME: *20 minutes*

Grilling Ingredients:

- 4 chicken breast halves, bone removed and skinless
- 1 tablespoon Malaysian Palm Fruit Oil
- 1 tablespoon raw coconut vinegar
- 1 garlic clove, finely chopped
- 1 teaspoon dried thyme leaves
- ½ teaspoon dried oregano leaves
- ½ teaspoon cayenne pepper
- ¼ teaspoon unrefined sea salt
- Dash pepper

Cooked Spinach Ingredients:

- 1 package (10 oz) fresh spinach, washed and leaves torn
- 1 medium green onion, minced
- 2 garlic cloves, finely chopped

- o 1 tablespoon Extra-virgin Olive Oil
- o ½ pound Fresh mushrooms, cut into slices

Directions:

1) Mix all the grilling ingredients together EXCEPT chicken in a bowl. Season the chicken with the well mixed grilling mixture.

2) On medium heat, allow to grill uncovered on each side for about 6-7 minutes.

3) In a skillet or saucepan, on medium heat, add palm oil, garlic and onions and stir-fry for about a minute. Add in the mushrooms and allow to cook for about 3½ minutes.

4) Mix in spinach and allow to cook for another 2 minutes. Remove and place cooked spinach on a serving dish then place the grilled chicken on top.

5) Serve equally and enjoy.

Happy Thanksgiving Turkey

Enjoying your Thanksgiving Turkey while you're on the Virgin Diet will be easy with this roast turkey. This turkey dish has a very rich flavor and is also quite juicy and moist. You may make this recipe whenever you want, it could even be perfect for Christmas.

Servings: *10*

PREPARATION TIME: *15 minutes*

COOKING TIME: *3 hours 10 minutes*

Ingredients:

- ¼ cup Extra-virgin Olive Oil, divided
- 1 (10 pound or 4.53 kg) turkey, washed and properly dried
- 1 tablespoon poultry seasoning
- 1 whole head garlic, top cut off
- 3 sprigs fresh thyme
- 2 lemon, cut in halves
- 1 sprig fresh rosemary
- 2 sprigs fresh sage
- 1 cup water
- Unrefined sea salt to taste
- Freshly ground pepper to taste

Directions:

1) Preheat your oven to 425 degrees Fahrenheit. Grease the bottom of a large roasting pan with 1 tablespoon coconut oil.

2) In a large bowl, add sea salt and pepper to the turkey and thoroughly season in the cavity and on the outside. Put the seasoned turkey in the roasting pan with the breast side up. Use a cooking brush to coat the turkey with the rest of the coconut oil.

3) Dash the poultry seasoning on the turkey, and thoroughly apply it into the skin with your hands. Put the whole garlic head, thyme, sage, 1 lemon half and rosemary inside the turkey's cavity. Add lemon juice from the remaining lemon half over the top of the seasoned turkey.

4) Place the seasoned turkey in the oven; add the cup of water to the bottom of the pan. Roast without the cover on for about an hour. Moisten the turkey with juices from the bottom of the pan after the first hour of cooking and cover it with foil if it appears too crispy brown.

5) Allow to bake for about another 2 hours. Take the turkey from the oven, and place on a turkey carving board. The turkey must be cooled for at least 10 minutes before carving. The skin should be removed while carving.

6) Strain the juice from the bottom of the pan into a medium saucepan. Add the juice of the remaining lemon halves to the juice in the saucepan and stir. Allow to reach boiling point and cook for about 8-10 minutes when the sauce thickens. Add more seasoning according to your taste.

7) Serve turkey with sauce and enjoy your meal. Happy thanksgiving!

Peas & Mushroom Chicken Thighs

This very easy and low calorie chicken recipe makes a great dinner or lunch. It has a good protein and fiber balance and goes great with salads or baked sweet potatoes.

Servings: *4*

PREPARATION TIME: *15 minutes*

COOKING TIME: *1 hour 5 minutes*

Ingredients:

4 chicken thighs, skinless

1½ teaspoon paprika

2 tablespoons raw coconut aminos

1 tablespoon Extra-virgin Olive Oil

½ teaspoon basil

1 teaspoon thyme leaves

¼ pound fresh mushrooms, sliced

½ cup reduced-sodium gluten free chicken broth

8 -10 ounces (about 283 grams) frozen peas, thawed and drained

Directions:

1) Preheat your oven to 350 degrees Fahrenheit.

2) Combine the following ingredients in a 2-qt casserole dish: paprika, coconut amino, olive oil, basil, and thyme. Add chicken thighs and cover well with seasoning mix.

3) Add sliced mushrooms and reduced-sodium chicken broth to the chicken thighs in the dish.

4) Place a lid on the casserole dish and bake for about 50-55 minutes. Add the fully thawed and drained peas, return lid and bake for another additional 12 minutes or until peas are cooked.

5) Remove casserole dish from the oven and serve as warm as possible. Enjoy.

Grilled Salmon with Salsa

This very interesting and flavorful salmon recipe is very nutritious. Coupled with the rich omega fatty acids in the salmon, you'll also get Vitamin A, Vitamin C, fiber, potassium and beta carotene nutrients from this meal. If you can't get nectarine, you may substitute it for peaches.

Servings: *2*

PREPARATION TIME: *15 minutes*

COOKING TIME: *10-12 minutes*

Ingredients:

- 12 ounces (2 pieces of 340 grams total) salmon fillet, without skin
- ½ teaspoon olive oil
- 1 tablespoon red onion, finely chopped
- 1 large nectarine, deseeded and finely chopped
- ½ small red pepper, chopped
- ½ red chili, finely chopped
- 1 tablespoon fresh lemon/lime juice
- ½ tablespoon fresh cilantro, finely chopped
- ½ tablespoon dried tarragon
- 3 tablespoons cold water
- ½ teaspoon unrefined sea salt, separated
- ¼ teaspoon ground black pepper

o   Vital Choice macadamia nut oil for greasing grill

Directions:

1) Prepare grill with cover and oil grill grate with Vital Choice macadamia nut oil. Apply medium grilling heat.

2) In a small bowl or cup, add red onion and cold water and allow to stand for about 8 minutes. In another bowl, add the following ingredients: red pepper, chili, lemon/lime juice, 1/8 teaspoon salt, nectarines, and cilantro. Mix well and place aside.

3) In a separate small bowl, add the following ingredients and mix together: ground black pepper, the remaining salt and tarragon. Brush salmon fillet with olive oil and coat both sides with the tarragon mixture.

4) Place seasoned salmon fillet on prepared hot grill grate. Place cover on grill and cook the salmon for about 5 minutes on each sides. After the salmon is entirely opaque, move it to a serving platter.

5) Drain the onion that was set aside of all water. Add the properly drained onion to the nectarine mixture and thoroughly combine. Evenly serve the nectarine salsa together with grilled salmon.

Salmon Grilay

Salmon is a very nutritious food and works well on the Virgin Diet. This is a quick and easy way to enjoy your salmon. Make this as often as you wish.

Servings: 4

PREPARATION TIME: 15 minutes

COOKING TIME: Under 15 minutes

Ingredients:

- 4 salmon fillets
- 2 teaspoons paprika
- 1 teaspoon chili powder
- ½ teaspoon ground cumin
- ½ teaspoon coconut palm sugar
- 1 teaspoon unrefined sea salt
- Vital Choice Macadamia Nut Oil

Directions:

1) Prepare your grill and heat it over medium heat.

2) Mix the following seasonings together: chili powder, paprika, ground cumin and coconut palm sugar. Sprinkle the salmon with salt and season with seasoning mixture.

3) Put seasoned salmon on heated grill rack coated with cooking spray; grill 7 minutes until fish flakes easily when tested with a fork.

CHAPTER 5

CYCLE 2 & 3 RECIPES

Hazelnut Cookie Pleasers

Yes, you can satisfy that sweet tooth with this protein-packed recipe! It has eggs in it which is one of the highly reactive foods.

Servings: *20 cookies*

PREPARATION TIME: *10 minutes*

COOKING TIME: *10-20 minutes*

Ingredients:

- o 1/3 cup coconut palm sugar
- o 2 egg whites
- o ½ cup walnuts, crushed
- o ¼ cup hazelnuts, chopped

Directions:

1) Place the sugar into a dry clean pan and put it into the warmed oven and switch off the heat. Leave it in the oven for approximately 10 minutes. Use the sugar when it is cooled.

2) Beat the egg whites until they form stiff peaks. Add in the oven-dry sugar gradually. Slowly fold in the nuts, while ensuring that the consistency of the egg whites is maintained.

3) Use a teaspoon to drop each cookie batter on a greased cookie sheet.

4) Preheat the oven to 400 degrees Fahrenheit. Switch off the oven and place in the cookies. Leave the cookies in the oven for a few hours (at least 2-3 hours) with the door closed.

5) Enjoy.

Feta Spinach Salad

Want something really healthy and easy? Then try this easy Feta Spinach recipe! It has dairy in it which is one of the highly reactive foods.

Servings: 2

PREPARATION TIME: *10 minutes*

COOKING TIME: *30 minutes*

Ingredients:

- o   1½ bunches fresh Spinach
- o   ½ cup crumbled feta cheese

Salad Dressing:

- o   ¼ teaspoon rosemary
- o   ¼ teaspoon thyme
- o   ½ teaspoon basil
- o   ½ teaspoon hyssop
- o   Unrefined sea salt and pepper to taste
- o   ½ tablespoon water
- o   1½ tablespoon lemon juice
- o   ½ cup Malaysian Palm fruit oil

Directions:

1) Wash the spinach thoroughly and drain in a colander. Tear it into bite-size pieces.

2) In a small bowl, mix the rosemary, thyme, hyssop, basil pepper and salt with water and allow it to stand for a few minutes.

3) Add the lemon juice and the palm oil to the mixture in the bowl. Then pour the dressing in a jar with a close-fitting cover and shake well.

4) In a bowl, lightly toss the spinach with the salad dressing and top with crumbled feta cheese. Serve right away and enjoy.

Berry Dream Smoothie

Try something new with this wonderful berry smoothie recipe! It has dairy in it which is one of the highly reactive foods

Servings: 1

PREPARATION TIME: *10 minutes*

COOKING TIME: *None*

Ingredients:

- o   1 cup Low Fat Milk
- o   ½ cup frozen Raspberries
- o   ½ cup frozen Blueberries
- o   1 cup Pak Choi
- o   1 tablespoon chia seeds (pre-soaked overnight or for at least 15 minutes)
- o   1 teaspoon Coconut Palm Sugar

Directions:

1) Place all ingredients into your high speed blender and process until smooth enough or for about a minute. Pour in a glass and serve.

Curried Fish Yogi

Enjoy this creamy salmon dish that has an irresistible flavor. It has dairy in it which is one of the highly reactive foods. This serves well with cooked brown rice or mixed salad.

Servings: 4

PREPARATION TIME: 15-20 minutes

COOKING TIME: 5-6 minutes

Ingredients:

- ½ pound (226 grams) salmon fillet
- 12 ounces (340 grams) whitefish fillet
- ¾ cup (about 226 grams or 8 ounces) peeled shrimp
- Gluten free chicken stock
- Unrefined sea salt and ground black pepper to taste
- ½ cup organic coconut mayonnaise
- 2 cups low-fat plain Greek yogurt
- 2 tsps. Curry powder
- Rind + juice of ½ lemon

For Garishing:

- A kiwifruit peeled and sliced
- Sprigs of fresh mint
- Flaked coconut

Directions:

1) Place the salmon and whitefish fillets in a shallow saucepan and add enough chicken stock to cover it.

2) Season to taste with salt and black pepper and simmer gently until cooked.

3) Carefully remove fish fillet from the chicken stock mixture and leave to cool a bit.

4) In a bowl, mix together the mayonnaise and the yogurt. Blend in the curry powder and lemon rind and juice.

5) Flake the cooked fish (not too fine) while removing any bones or skin. Mix the flaked fish into the curry sauce, along with the shrimp.

6) Arrange the curried fish yogi on serving plates and garnish with slices of kiwi, mint and coconut flakes.

Egg and Veggie Frinny

You can have a delightful dish out of simple veggies and eggs too! Try this recipe! It has egg in it which is one of the highly reactive foods.

Servings: 2

PREPARATION TIME: 10 minutes

COOKING TIME: 15 minutes

Ingredients:

- 2 eggs, beaten
- 2 carrots, chopped
- 2 zucchini, chopped
- 2 spring onions, chopped
- Fresh coriander
- 3 tbsp of extra virgin coconut oil
- 1 tsp of black pepper
- 1 tsp of cumin
- A handful of kale, chopped
- 2 red chilies, chopped
- 1 tsp of unrefined sea salt

Directions:

1) In a mixing bowl, add the eggs.

2) Add the remaining ingredients and thoroughly mix together.

3) In a pan, heat the oil.

4) Now pour in the batter.

5) Fry it golden brown.

6) Serve with appropriate diet friendly dipping sauce.

Spacado Smoothie

Spinach and avocado are among the healthiest foods on the planet, now you can enjoy the health benefits of these simple ingredients with this recipe! It has soy in it which is one of the highly reactive foods.

Servings: 1

PREPARATION TIME: *10 minutes*

COOKING TIME: *None*

Ingredients:

- o   1 cup Soy Milk
- o   1 cup frozen Mixed Berries
- o   ¼ cup Avocado, diced or cubed or ½ of a ripe Avocado
- o   ½ cup Spinach
- o   ¼ teaspoon Flaxseed, ground

Directions:

- o   Place all ingredients into your high speed blender and process until smooth enough or for about a minute. Pour in a glass and serve.

Shrimpy Green Peas Stir-Fry

Enjoy this quick and easy to prepare dish plus great nutritional benefits. It has <u>gluten</u> in it which is one of the highly reactive foods. This serves well with cooked brown rice.

Servings: 2-3

PREPARATION TIME: *10 minutes*

COOKING TIME: *10 minutes*

Ingredients:

- ¾ pounds (340 grams) peeled shrimp
- 1 tbsp. Extra-virgin coconut oil
- ½ -inch piece of fresh ginger, peeled then finely chopped
- 1 garlic clove, peeled then finely chopped
- 1 large green onion
- 1 leek, white part only, cut into strips
- ¼ cup green peas, shelled
- 1½ cups bean sprouts
- 1 tbsp. raw coconut aminos
- ½ tsp. brown sugar
- Unrefined sea salt to taste

Directions:

1) In a wok, heat the oil and stir-fry the shrimp for about 3 minutes. Place the shrimp aside.

2) Reheat the oil and add ginger and garlic. Stir quickly, then add the following: green peas, onion and leeks. Stir-fry for approximately 3 minutes.

3) Add the bean sprouts and shrimp to the already cooked vegetables. Stir in the raw coconut aminos, brown sugar, and sea salt. Cook for 2 minutes.

4) Serve as warm as possible.

Veggie Nut Lettuce Wrap

The healthiest lettuce wrap you would ever eat! Try it today. It has peanut in it which is one of the highly reactive foods.

Servings: *2*

PREPARATION TIME: *10 minutes*

COOKING TIME: *5 minutes*

Ingredients:

A handful of lettuce

2 carrots, chopped

2 avocado, chopped

2 apples, chopped

½ cup of almond, chopped

½ cup of peanuts chopped

1 tsp of cinnamon

1 tsp of pepper

1 tsp of unrefined sea salt

Directions:

1) In a bowl, combine all the ingredients nicely except the lettuce.

2) Now place the lettuces in a plate.

3) Pour in the mixture in the middle.

4) Wrap up the lettuces real tightly.

5) Serve fresh with any dipping sauce.

Spicy Ginger Salmon Steak

Enjoy this extraordinary salmon steak dish. It has dairy in it which is one of the highly reactive foods.

Servings: *4*

PREPARATION TIME: *15 minutes*

COOKING TIME: *12-15 minutes*

Ingredients:

- 4 salmon steaks, about an inch thick
- ½ cup coconut palm sugar
- 1 tbsp. ground allspice
- 1 tbsp. mustard powder
- 1 tbsp. grated fresh ginger
- 1 cucumber, peeled, deseeded and cut into long quarters cut into 1-inch pieces
- 1 bunch green onions, roots trimmed and most of green part removed
- 2 tbsps. Butter
- 1 tbsp. lemon juice
- 2 tsps. chopped fresh dill weed
- 1 tbsp. chopped fresh parsley
- Unrefined sea salt and black pepper to taste

Directions:

1) Combine the sugar and spices together and rub the mixture into the surface of both sides of the salmon steaks. It is best to allow the seasoned steaks to marinate for at least an hour in the refrigerator.

2) In the meantime, place the cucumber and green onions into a saucepan, along with the seasoning, butter, lemon juice, dill, seasoning and fresh parsley.

3) Cook over a moderate heat for approximately 10 minutes or until cucumber is cooked.

4) Place the salmon steaks under a preheated moderate broiler and cook for about 5-6 minutes on both sides.

5) Serve on a serving platter with cucumber and green onion. Enjoy.

Sweet Potato Supreme Smoothie

Sweet potatoes are just some sweet darlings! Enjoy this tasty and nutritious sweet potato virgin smoothie and be comforted. It has gluten in it which is one of the highly reactive foods.

Servings: 1

PREPARATION TIME: *10 minutes*

COOKING TIME: *None*

Ingredients:

- o   1 cup organic unsweetened Coconut Milk
- o   ¼ cup Rolled Whole Oats
- o   ¼ cup Sweet Potato, cooked and chilled
- o   2 teaspoon Cinnamon Powder or Nutmeg Powder
- o   1 teaspoon Vanilla Extract
- o   3 Ice Cubes

Directions:

1. Place all ingredients into your high speed blender and process until smooth enough or for about a minute. Pour in a glass and serve.

Greek Plum Smoothie

This is a favorite healthy smoothie. It's naturally creamy and supports a healthy heart. It has dairy in it which is one of the highly reactive foods.

Servings: 1

PREPARATION TIME: *10 minutes*

COOKING TIME: *None*

Ingredients:

- o   3 Red Plums, cut in halves & seeds removed
- o   ½ cup frozen Stawberries
- o   ½ cup fat-free plain Greek Yogurt
- o   ¼ cup Organic unsweetened Coconut Milk
- o   ¼ teaspoon ground Flax Seeds
- o   A dash of grated Nutmeg

Directions:

1) Place all ingredients into your high speed blender and process until smooth enough or for about a minute. Pour in a glass and serve.

Toasty Egg in Almond Flavor

Why not feel the taste of Arabia with a very simple recipe that takes less than 45 min to prepare. It has egg in it which is one of the highly reactive foods.

Servings: *2*

PREPARATION TIME: *10 minutes*

COOKING TIME: *30 minutes*

Ingredients:

- o 1 cup of almond flour
- o 4 eggs
- o ½ cup of gluten free bread crumbs
- o 1 tsp of paprika
- o 1 tsp of white pepper
- o 1 tsp of allspice
- o Malaysian Palm Fruit Oil
- o 1 tsp of unrefined sea salt

Directions:

1) In a bowl, throw in the flour.
2) Add the spices.
3) Add the oil and mix until the mixture is smooth.
4) Now in muffin tray grease some oil.

5) Pour in the mixture.

6) Bake for nearly 20 minutes over 180C.

7) Now take out your tray and let it cool.

8) Once it is cool, take few portions out of the baked bread to put the eggs.

9) Pour in one egg in each middle.

10) Again bake for 5 minutes and serve hot.

Lamb Kabab

Try this aromatic and healthy Lamb dish at home now. It has egg in it which is one of the highly reactive foods.

Servings: 2

PREPARATION TIME: 20 minutes

COOKING TIME: 10 minutes

Ingredients:

- 1 pound (453 gram) of lamb
- 2 eggs, beaten
- 2 tbsp of coconut flour
- 2 tbsp of rice flour
- 2 tbsp of coconut flour
- 6 spring onions, diced
- 4 garlic cloves, diced
- 1 tsp of clove powder
- 1 tsp of allspice
- Chopped bell pepper, according to taste
- 4 tbsp of extra virgin coconut oil (for the mixture)
- 3 tbsp of Olive oil (for frying)
- Unrefined Sea Salt to taste
- Fresh parsley, chopped

Directions:

1) In a large bowl, throw in all of your ingredients.

2) Mix them well.

3) Pour them into a good food processor.

4) Blend until the mixture is smooth.

5) Make flat balls out of them.

6) Now heat the olive oil into a pan and fry them golden brown from both sides.

7) Serve hot with a diet friendly dipping sauce.

Fried Tilapia in Nuts

Treat your-self today with a very easy-to-follow recipe that tastes as good as it looks on the plate. It has peanut in it which is one of the highly reactive foods.

Servings: *2*

PREPARATION TIME: *10 minutes*

COOKING TIME: *30 minutes*

Ingredients:

- o   2 Tilapia fish
- o   ½ cup of peanuts
- o   ½ cup of tomato puree
- o   ½ cup of walnuts
- o   2 tbsp of Malaysian Palm Fruit Oil
- o   2 tbsp of ginger garlic paste (or 1 tbsp. minced garlic and 1 tbsp. minced ginger)
- o   1 tsp of red chili paste
- o   1 tsp of turmeric powder
- o   Unrefined sea salt and pepper to taste
- o   1 tsp of lime juice

Directions:

1) In a bowl, marinate the tilapia with the puree, the pastes, the spices, the salt, the turmeric powder and 1 tsp of oil.
2) Now put in the freeze for 10 minutes.
3) In a baking tray, grease some oil.
4) Plate the fish and throw in all the nuts on top.
5) Drizzle some more oil on top.
6) Bake for nearly 30 minutes and serve hot.

Salmon Capri

Enjoy this tasty sautéed salmon dish with coconut vinegar sauce. It has <u>*gluten*</u> *in it which is one of the highly reactive foods.*

Servings: *2*

PREPARATION TIME: *15-25 minutes*

COOKING TIME: *25 minutes*

Ingredients:

- o 1 pound (453 grams) salmon steak or fillets, skin removed and cut into 1-inch pieces
- o 2 tbsp white flour
- o Unrefined sea salt and ground black pepper to taste
- o 1 small carrot, peeled and sliced thinly
- o 1 small onion, sliced thinly
- o A bay leaf
- o 1 sprig parsley
- o 1/8 fresh red chili, finely chopped
- o ½ cup raw coconut vinegar
- o 2 garlic cloves
- o Malaysian Palm Fruit Oil
- o 1/3 cup water

Directions:

1) Mix the sea salt and black pepper with the flour. Dredge the salmon fillets or steaks in this flour mixture, while shaking off any excess flour.

2) On medium heat, fry in Malaysian Palm Fruit oil until a golden brown color is achieved on all sides. Remove from pan and drain excess oil on paper towels.

3) To the frying pan, add in the carrots and onion and allow to cook for about 5 minutes. Then add in the bay leaf, parsley, coconut vinegar, chili pepper and water. Add salt if needed. Cover the frying pan with a lid and allow to simmer for about 15-20 minutes.

4) Place the browed salmon fillets in a small-medium casserole dish and pour coconut vinegar sauce over it. Sprinkle with the sliced garlic and cover securely. Leave in the refrigerator for at least 2 hours (24 hour is best) turning the salmon fillets occasionally.

5) For serving, remove the salmon fillets from the sauce and arrange on a serving platter. Pour the sauce over the salmon fillet and top with parsley, if preferred.

CHAPTER 6

USEFUL LIST OF FOOD SUBSTITUTES

Having a handy list of Virgin Diet friendly food substitutes will help to make your healthy lifestyle and food choices much easier. This list can be used to ensure that you use the right ingredients at all times. You should also note that depending on the expected outcome of your recipe, some of these substitutes may or may not work. This list is great for those who have favorites or those who like to experiment with different recipes.

MY LIST OF RECOMMENDED SUBSTITUTES:

1) **White rice substitute** = brown rice

2) **Brown sugar substitute** = coconut palm sugar, monkfruit, stevia, cinnamon, vanilla

3) **Cornstarch substitute** = arrowroot powder

4) **Regular salt substitute** = unrefined sea salt

5) **Regular oatmeal substitute** = gluten-free oatmeal

6) **Dairy butter or margarine substitute** = cashew butter, almond butter, macadamia nut butter

7) **Soy sauce** = raw coconut aminos

8) **Dairy milk substitute** = organic unsweetened coconut milk

9) **Peanut substitutes** = walnut, almonds, hazelnuts, cashews

10) **Vinegar substitute** = raw coconut vinegar

11) **Dairy yogurt** = coconut yogurt

12) **Soy milk substitute** = organic unsweetened coconut milk

13) **Cooking oil substitutes** = Vital choice macadamia nut oil, Extra-virgin coconut oil, Malaysian palm fruit oil, Extra-virgin olive oil

14) **Egg substitute** = 1 tablespoon of chia seeds combined with 3 tablespoons of water and allowed to soak for about 15 minutes.

15) **White flour substitute** = flaxseed meal, almond flour, coconut flour

CHAPTER 7

CONCLUSION

Embracing positive change is one sure way of making progress. By purchasing this book, you've shown that you are serious about making progress where your health is concerned. That, by itself, is commendable. With that being said, the only thing between you and your weight loss success and healthy lifestyle goal is you. By using my recipes and sticking to the other Virgin Diet strategies you'll soon realize that being overweight doesn't have to be a permanent condition. You can turn things around and obtain an ideal weight. If I have done it, so can you.

So many times, dieters are steaming with enthusiasm at the beginning of a weight loss program. But obviously, if we are serious about losing weight or achieving anything else, consistency will be essential for success. You have to stick with the program in order to realize the benefits. It's that simple. With the information in this book, you will always have knowledge to take control of your weight and your overall health.

I'm delighted to know that I have been able to assist you in achieving better health. I'm also happy to know that I've been able to ultimately contribute to your longevity. Even if you drift a bit from this diet and gain unwanted weight, years from now, you will still be equipped with the recipes and information you've received in this book. Consequently, you will be able to turn your situation around whenever you wish. Always remember that staying healthy is ALWAYS your best option.

Ultimately, your own healthier lifestyle can be as easy or as difficult as you make it. Undoubtedly, you deserve to live a life of good health.

All the best,

Stacy